CURLING
Handbook

FOR
RLERS, TEACHERS & COACHES

by
ROY D. THIESSEN

hancock
house

SAANICHTON, TORONTO, SEATTLE

ISBN 0-919654-71-1

 Copyright © 1977   Roy D. Thiessen

Cataloging in Publication Data

Thiessen, Roy D 1935-
    Curling handbook for curlers, teachers, and
coaches.

    Bibliography: p.
    1. Curling. I. Title.
GV845.T46 796.9'6 77-2578
ISBN 0-919654-71-1

Designed by NICHOLAS NEWBECK DESIGN

Published by:

Hancock House Publishers Ltd.

3215 Island View Road
SAANICHTON, B.C. V0S 1M0

Hancock House Publishers Inc.

12008 1st Avenue South
SEATTLE, WA. 98168

Foreword

The quality of leadership given to an athletic program determines to a great extent its success. The coach has a marked influence on the players. Therefore, it is desirable to examine the effective practices that have been developed by a successful teacher and coach for carrying out the job at hand—to teach the skills of curling, stimulate interest and enjoyment in the game for its participants while, at the same time, having an organizational approach that assures success.

During the past 16 years I have had the pleasure of observing the teaching practices and philosophy of the author through his work with high school students. Within the high school and junior curling program Mr. Roy Thiessen has been eminently successful. During the past decade teams tutored by him either won or reached the finals in all but two championships. This speaks highly of the approach taken to teach the game to young players, and the continuity of his program.

This handbook was developed from Roy's school program, his graduate research and practice at the community level through hundreds of clinics conducted by him. Prospective teachers and coaches too often feel inadequate in their knowledge and skills of curling and they shy away from the very thought of teaching it. The purpose of this book is to help solve group and individual instructional problems. The aim is to furnish the conscientious teacher with sound material and teaching methods. I believe that any dedicated tutor with the desire to teach curling will succeed in doing so by following this guide.

I take pleasure and pride in commending this work to teachers and coaches for better curling.

Gordon E. Mundle,
Executive Secretary,
Saskatchewan High Schools
Athletic Association.

Acknowledgements

For their helpful and sound suggestions in the preparation of this book, the author expresses most sincere thanks to Bob McWhirter of Regina for his assistance in technique study; Garald Bowie of Washington State University for his extensive research into the history of curling; Dr. R. Webster of Michigan State University for his technical assistance.

Appreciation also goes to the many Moose Jaw Junior curlers who have dedicated their time and efforts to the sport of curling as both curlers and instructors. A special thanks to Carol Rudd and Julie Burke, Canadian Junior Champions, 1970, and Randy Thiessen for their practical assistance by posing for instructional photographs.

Lastly, the author extends thanks to his wife Starla and his children Heather and Gregory for their help, encouragement and toleration which enabled him to produce this book.

Contents

To the enthusiastic and loyal curlers who have dedicated themselves to the sport as participants, clinicians and instructors to bring curling to its rightful place alongside the other sports of our schools, clubs and colleges throughout the country.

1.
Introduction to Coaching

The success of curling teams generally depends upon their mastery of the fundamentals of the game and attitude toward competition. It is the coach's responsibility through continual analysis to develop necessary fundamentals and attitudes to best prepare his team for competition. The coach's philosophy is the foundation upon which his success depends. It must be in conformance with his philosophy of life, of government and of education. He must recognize his responsibilities as a teacher of youth as well as a coach. By his leadership he will set an example for sound living habits and develop, to an extent, the individual personality of his team members. He must teach them to meet adversity as well as success, ingrain in them the spirit of sportsmanship, cultivate moral integrity as well as physical development and prepare each team member to become a team member of society.

An important factor in the philosophy of a coach is his attitude toward winning and losing. A coach assumes responsibilities beyond fielding a winning team. He is charged with guiding mental and physical development. He must realize that his attitude and philosophy are reflected in his team members. His perspectives and his objectives must be balanced and defined to himself. If a coach blames defeat on anything and everything but himself, his players will be inclined to excuse their bad individual performances by pointing the finger of defeat to someone or something else. A coach leads by example; he should be sure his leadership sets a good example.

Each coach coaches to win; his team plays to achieve the same result. A coach attempts to inculcate a winning spirit within the group that will enable his team to meet its competition more favorably. He wants his squad, individually and collectively, to have the quality of pride of achievement. He wants a sense of humility, generous yet humble in success, strong in failure. Both success and adversity must be met with stability. If the athlete experiences only victory during his competitive career, he will be poorly prepared for life. The coach's philosophy must be all-inclusive. It cannot pertain only to the things he would like to have happen.

In general the coach must be willing to give freely of his time and often of his money, his energy, his youth, his family life, and sometimes even his health. In return, he must expect little financial reward, little comfort, little privacy, little praise, and some criticism. However, he may expect to reap a great deal of personal satisfaction. If he is a good coach, he is respected in his community, admired by his players and makes lasting friends in his field. He has the satisfaction of seeing his players develop and improve in ability; he knows the thrill of victory and learns to accept defeat with grace.

Curling is a game for all ages and thus can be enjoyed by participants throughout their lifetime. The enjoyment and ease with which one participates is dependent upon the fundamental skill one possesses. Thus the need for a clear, concise approach to the learning of the fundamentals is most essential. It is the writer's hope that the succeeding material will aid the coach, instructor and curler, male and female alike, to become more proficient at the game of curling.

2.
History of Curling in North America

The early history of many games is obscure and fragmented; and the origin of curling, today one of the popular sports in Scotland, England, Wales, United States, Canada, Sweden, Switzerland, New Zealand, Norway, Italy, Austria, France, China and Australia, is shrouded by the mists of antiquity that the origin of the game has been for many generations a subject of continuous controversy between rival schools of thought (Royal Caledonian Curling Club, 1961, p. 32).

Two basic theories exist in regard to the origin of the game. One is that it was brought to Scotland during the reign of James I (1394-1439) by the Flemings who emigrated to Britain from the Low Countries of Europe. The other is that curling originated in Scotland.

It appears that curling as it is now known is more a matter of evolution rather than that of invention. It thus seems that the modern-day version of the game of curling had its beginning in Scotland. The earliest references to the game date back to the 1500's. The first evidence found in Scotland was in the form of a curling stone or "Kuting" stone with the following inscription, "St. Js. B. Stirling 1511."

In 1842 Queen Victoria placed her blessing on the Grand Caledonian Curling Club (originated in 1838) and it thus became the Royal Caledonian Curling Club which has since become the "mother" club to all curlers throughout the world. Much of the development and expansion of the game of curling is due to the Royal Caledonian Curling Club.

Curling in Canada

It is believed that the game of curling was brought to Canada by the Scottish Regiments in 1759. The first North American club to be organized was the Royal Montreal Curling Club in 1807. In 1841 the Canadian branch of the Grand Caledonian Club was established with headquarters in Montreal. It was recognized as the governing body for curling in Canada.

Following Confederation in 1867, the curling fraternity felt a need for unity and thus steps were taken to form a Dominion Curling Association, which degenerated to the formation of the Ontario branch of the Royal Caledonian Club (later the Ontario Curling Association). From Ontario curling moved west and Winnipeg, Manitoba, became the western headquarters.

It was not until 1935 that the Dominion Curling Association became a reality with New Brunswick, Northern Ontario, Ontario, Manitoba, Saskatchewan, Alberta and Crow's Nest Pass joined together under the leadership of John T. Haig of Winnipeg, Manitoba. In its first year Association membership consisted of 530 clubs with a total of 18,301 registered members. The rules of the Royal Caledonian Curling Club of Scotland were adopted. In the second year of existence Prince Edward Island and British Columbia joined the Dominion Association. Quebec followed suit in 1943. Their delay was due to the fact that a large part of their membership curled with iron stones rather than granite stones, thus they found it difficult to compete with the rest of the Associations of the Dominion. In 1944 Nova Scotia officially joined the "mother" club. The truly national representation became a reality in 1950 when Newfoundland, the tenth province, joined the Dominion Curling Association of Canada.

The MacDonald Brief Championship, begun in 1927, has become the playdown, emblematic of curling supremacy in Canada.

HIGH SCHOOL CURLING

The first organized high school boys curling took place in Manitoba in 1939 with a high school boys Christmas Bonspiel. Saskatchewan and Alberta followed suit and a Western Prairies Championship was staged at Regina, Saskatchewan in 1947. In 1949 a Dominion Playdown was organized with nine provinces competing. Ontario was divided into two areas, thus ten teams competed for Dominion supremacy. Newfoundland has since joined to become the eleventh entry.

High school girls curling is currently carried to a provincial championship in Saskatchewan and Alberta.

LADIES CURLING

Ladies curling, since the first ladies competition in 1914 in the Manitoba Curling Club Bonspiel, has become most popular in North America. The first ladies Association dates back to 1925 with the formation of the Manitoba Ladies Curling Association. The first ladies curling championship was hosted by Regina, Saskatchewan in 1953. Alberta, Saskatchewan and Manitoba

11

participated. In 1960 the Canadian Ladies Curling Association was organized and the Dominion Diamond "D" Championship became emblematic of National curling supremacy.

MIXED CURLING

"With entries from every province, the O'Keefe National Mixed Championship got off to a running start (in 1964) and the outlook for the future is rosy" (The Curler, 1964, p. 18). Thus mixed curling has proven most popular and is a highlight event of the yearly Canada-wide competition.

JUNIOR CURLING

A junior men's and ladies competition has recently been developed. Competition is open to those under the age of 20. Uniroyal of Canada sponsored the first truly World Junior Men's Championship in Windsor, Ontario, in 1974. The Junior Ladies Canadian Championship began in 1972.

CURLING IN THE UNITED STATES

It was in the 1830's that the game of curling crept across the Canadian border into northern Michigan and the New England States. The first club organized in the United States was the Orchard Lake Club of Detroit in 1831. The first Association to be formed to represent the American curlers was the Grand National Curling Club in 1867.

In 1945 the Midwest Curling Association was established and presently covers Nebraska, Wisconsin, Ohio, Illinois and Michigan. In 1958 the United States Curling Association was incorporated to promote curling and unite into one association the men's curling organizations throughout the United States of America. Its present membership consists of the Grand National, Midwest, Minnesota State, North Dakota, Washington State, and Alaska Curling Associations.

LADIES CURLING

The United States Women's Curling Association was organized in 1950 with a membership of 36 clubs.

Since the modernization of the game there has been a general re-awakening of curling in North America. It has ever increasingly become a game for young and old, male and female alike. With the use of artificial ice, heated curling rinks and improved skills, curling is fast finding its place in the field of winter sports in North America.

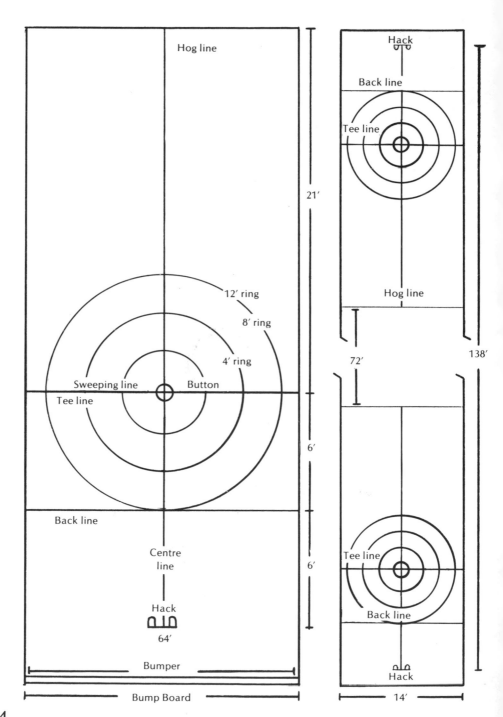

14

Terminology of Curling

Curling, like many other sports, has a vocabulary unique to the game itself. Thus it is necessary to define the terms used to describe the playing surface, techniques and methodology related to the game of curling.

Back-boards: Boards or bumper at the ends of each sheet of ice.

Back-ring: The portion of the 8-foot and 12-foot rings behind the tee-line.

Biter: A rock partially inside the outer edge of the 12-foot ring.

Blank End: An end that is scoreless, with no rocks in the house at completion of the end.

Blanking an End: A deliberate attempt by a skip with last rock advantage to create a blank end to retain last rock advantage in the succeeding end.

Bonspiel: A curling competition comprised of a number of individual events.

Bumper:	Is the backstop (foam or rubber composition) which rests against the back-boards to protect them from impact of rocks.
Bumpboard Weight:	A rock that has just enough momentum to reach the bumper.
Burned Rock:	A delivered rock touched by a team member or his equipment while the rock is in motion.
Bury a Stone:	A rock placed behind a guard or guards so that it cannot be hit directly.
Button:	The area within the center ring.
Chip:	A shot that hits another rock on the side.
Chip and roll:	To hit an opposing rock and roll to a new position in the house.
Coming Home:	The final end of regulation play of a match.
Counter:	Any rock which touches any portion of the house.

Dead Weight: A rock with sufficient momentum to come to the face of or "freeze" to a rock in the house.

Double: Removal of two rocks from the playing area with one shot.

Draw: The lateral movement of a rock caused by the turning of the handle.

Draw Weight: Sufficient momentum to enable a rock delivered to reach the house.

End: That portion of a game when 16 rocks have been played. A Game consists of a specified number of ends of play (usually 10).

Extra End: An additional end played to break a tie.

Fall: A portion of the ice surface which is not level and thus causes a moving rock to deviate from its normal path opposite to its rotation.

Freeze: A rock with sufficient momentum to come to the face of another rock in the house, without moving it.

17

Front-ring: The portion of 8-foot and 12-foot rings in front of the tee-line.

Giving Ice: The placing of the broom for a target to aim at, in regard to the amount of draw expected.

Guard: Any rock that blocks the path of another rock.

Hack: Foot-hold from which the rock is delivered.

Hack Weight: Sufficient momentum to move a rock from hack to hack.

Heavy: A rock delivered with more than desired weight.

Heavy Ice: Dull ice, thus requires more effort to deliver a rock.

Hog Line: Line 21 feet in front of the tee-line. The rocks must completely cross the hog line in order to be considered in play.

House: The area within the 12-foot circle.

Ice: The distance between the skip's broom and the

	rock or target area, determined by the amount of "draw" anticipated.
In-turn:	A clockwise rotation imparted to the rock as it is released in the delivery (right-handed curler).
Keen Ice:	Fast ice.
Last Rock:	The last rock to be delivered in an end.
Lead:	The first player on the team. He delivers the first rock of each end.
Light:	A rock that is delivered with less than the desired weight.
Lost turn:	A rock which has lost its initial rotation.
Narrow:	A rock delivered inside the imaginary line to the skip's broom.
Off the Broom:	A rock delivered off the imaginary line to the skip's broom.
On the Broom:	A rock delivered on the imaginary line to the skip's broom.

Out-turn: A counterclockwise rotation imparted to the rock as it is released in the delivery (right-handed curler).

Pebble: The rough playing surface caused by sprinkling water on the ice.

Playdown: A series of competitions to declare a champion.

Port: An opening between two rocks wide enough to allow another rock to pass through.

Raise: When one rock is bumped ahead with another.

Rock: Curling stone used by a player.

Roll: The movement of the hitting rock after hitting a stationary rock in play.

Runner: A fast-moving rock with negligible "draw."

Runs: Small ridges or hollows in the ice causing the rock to deviate from the normal path.

Second: The second player on

the team. He delivers the second pair of rocks.

Sheet: The ice surface upon which a match is played.

Shot Rock: The rock nearest the center of the rings.

Skip: The last member of the curling team, who generally delivers the last pair of rocks and also directs the strategy of the match.

Stone: Curling rock used by a player.

Straight Handle: A rock without in-turn or out-turn rotation.

Sweeping: To sweep in front of a moving rock with broom or brush.

Swingy Ice: Ice on which the "draw" of a rock is greater than normal.

Take-out: A removal of a rock from the playing area by hitting it with another rock delivered with sufficient momentum to do so.

Tee Line: Line passing through the center of the circles at right angles to the center line.

Third: The vice-skip. The player who delivers the third pair of rocks.

Vice-Skip: The third player of a team.

Weight: The amount of momentum imparted to a rock in delivery.

Wick: When a rock hits the edge of a stationary rock, so that the thrown rock continues in motion.

Wide: A rock delivered outside the imaginary line to the skip's broom.

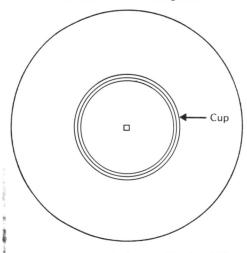

Bottom View of Curling Rock

← Cup

Maximum   Weight: 44 lbs.

The Curling Rock

Handle

Goose Neck

Leather Washer

Striking Edge

Running Surface

Bolt

Cup: The concave portion of the curling rock. The rock rides on the edge of the cup, thus reducing the area of surface contact with the ice.

Maximum Circumference 36'

22

Curling Equipment

The advent of heated indoor curling rinks has had a great effect upon equipment used by the curler. The curling hat has become optional. Gloves are essential and for greatest comfort and protection against blisters, a tightly fitting pair of unlined leather gloves are recommended. A curling sweater or waist length jacket or sweater should be worn along with a pair of slacks which allow the curler to comfortably get down into the curler's delivery position. The most satisfactory type of slacks are the stretching type now especially made for curlers.

Footwear is extremely important to the curler. First, the curler must have full freedom of movement of the ankle. The footwear must give the curler sound footing on ice but on the other hand also allow the curler to slide in the delivery of the curling rock. Thus it has been common practice to wear a non-slip substance on the right shoe and use a smooth surface on the left sole to reduce the friction when sliding. It is highly recommended that beginning curlers acquire proper footwear in order to develop a sound delivery technique. As the beginner becomes more confident and proficient in the sliding delivery technique, a plastic sole may be used to reduce the friction against the ice surface. The rubber soled right foot is most important, firstly in order to help in the maintenance of balance and, second, for traction when moving on the ice to sweep the curling rocks. Crepe sole is also commonly used on the right shoe. If the curler uses the plastic or tile-like material on the sliding shoe, he is well advised to have a toe rubber to slip onto it when not in use and thus preserve the smooth finish for a longer period of time.

The curling broom is an important part of the curler's equipment. The curler should select a broom that he or she can readily use. Most of the corn brooms are sold in three weights, light, medium and heavy weights. It is just as important that a curler does not use a broom which is too light, as it is for him to try to use one which is too heavy. For most effective sweeping results, the curler must have to apply effort to make the broom snap. The new nylon synthetic brooms on market now are adjustable in regard to flexibility. The length of the broom handle is relative to the weight of the broom, thus should not be altered as it will adversely affect the sweeping action of the broom. It is important to realize that each individual must have a broom which best suits his or her particular body size and strength.

The Scottish brush is becoming more and more popular in our North American game. Scottish curlers have used it for many years. The brush is usually made of horse hair, Mexican fibre or flagged polypropylene. It is the author's opinion that the brush is at least as effective as the American corn broom when used in sweeping draw shots or soft take-out shots, but seems to lose some of the effectiveness on the running take-out shots because it is difficult to do an effective job and keep up with the rock at the same time. The novice curler can probably be more effective with the brush than the broom, in that it is easier to keep the path in front of the moving rock free of debris.

Generally speaking North American curlers have led the way in the development of a wide variety of curling equipment for the curling enthusiast. Manufacturers have placed on the market a wide selection of curling gloves, sweaters, shoes, slacks and brooms from which to choose. The matched team sweaters and slacks have done much to add color and glamour to the roaring game of curling.

5.
Description and Rules of Curling

This chapter is intended to give briefly to the novice some of the important aspects of the game, and it is hoped that it will help to give a better understanding of the study.

A rink or team consists of four players, each handling two rocks, making a total of eight rocks played by each team during an end. Rocks are played alternately with those of the opposition.

A goal in the form of a 12-foot circle at each end of the long narrow sheet of ice is called the "house." As in shuffle-board, an end has been completed when all 16 rocks have been played to the opposite end of the sheet. Then, for convenience, the next end is played in the opposite direction to the other house. Any number of ends may be played but the number is agreed upon in advance. Normally 10 ends are played, which takes about two and one-half hours.

The player uses a hack for his foot at the end of the sheet of ice from which the rocks are delivered. The hack is fastened to the ice to keep him from slipping as he swings the rock back and then forward on its journey down the ice.

The first player to throw his two rocks is called the lead. After the lead has delivered his two rocks, alternately with the opposing lead, it is then the second player's turn to perform likewise (he is called the second man). Having finished delivering his rocks, the lead moves up to take over sweeping duties with the number three player, who is called the third man or vice-skip and has already helped in the sweeping of the first two lead rocks for his side. In turn, the third plays his two rocks alternately with the opposing team's third. His two rocks are swept by the lead and second. The fourth player is called the skip, and he is last to throw his two rocks while the lead and second sweep and the third takes over the skip's duties. Except while delivering his two rocks, the skip remains in the house at the opposite end where he plans strategy and directs the play of his team. He decides which shots to play and controls sweeping for his team.

As each team takes its turn alternately, the opposing four players give up the ice to the team whose rock is being played, since they are not allowed to interfere in any way with the opponents' rocks. The opposing skip, however, may remain behind the house, in order to watch the opposition rock and study the ice and action of the rock. He may also sweep opposing rocks after they cross the tee line.

One must understand the purpose of that all-important feature of the game, sweeping. A rock, which otherwise would fall short of the house or intended destination, can be brought along to its proper destination by accurate sweeping. Studies have shown that a rock can be made to travel as much as ten feet farther by vigorous sweeping. A well-swept rock will not arc, or curl, as much; therefore it can be made to pass a guard rock which would otherwise be wicked.

Curling rocks do not travel in a straight line. As they are delivered they are made to rotate by turning the handle as the release is made, either to the right (in turn) or the left (out turn). In calling for a given play, the skip first pats the ice with his broom, indicating where he wants the rock to end up. Then, after signaling for the desired turn, he puts the broom down as a target for the player, judging the amount of "draw" needed to have the rock reach the objective or accomplish the intended purpose.

The score for the end is determined by the opposing thirds who must agree or call for an umpire's decision. As in the game of horseshoes only the rocks that are nearest the center of the rings count. For example, one side has two rocks nearer the center than any of the opponent's rocks, the count is two; nothing for the opponent. The rule is that the winning team of an end must play the first rock of the next end, thereby giving an advantage to the side that lost the previous end. To determine the team that throws first at the beginning of the game, a coin is tossed.

RULES

The rules established under the Royal Caledonian Curling Club are adopted by the rest of the curling associations throughout the world. The rules that appear here are summarized for the sake of brevity.

Rule 3   Deals with dimensions and markings of a sheet of curling ice as outlined on page 14.

Rule 4(2)   No rock shall exceed 44 pounds in weight, including the handles.

Rule 4(3)   Should a rock break, the largest fragment shall count.

Rule 4(4)   Any rock which rolls over shall not count.

28

Rule 4 (5)   Should the handle quit the rock in delivery, the player shall be entitled to replay the rock.

Rule 4 (6)   A rock must clear the "hog line" to remain in play unless it strikes another rock first. Any rock completely crossing over the "back line" is out of play.

Rule 5 (1)   Each rink shall consist of four players, each player delivering two rocks alternately with his opponent. This rotation of players shall not change once the match has begun.

Rule 5 (4)   The vice-skip shall settle by lot which party shall lead at the first end and thereafter the winners of the preceding end shall lead (including extra ends).

5 (5)   If the skip, vice-skip, or second is absent, the lead shall play four rocks. If the lead is absent, the second shall play four rocks.

Rule 6   The skip shall have control of the game for his rink, and may play any position in the game he elects, but without changing his position once the match has commenced. When his turn to play comes, he shall select one of his players to act as skip.

Rule 7 (1)   During the course of a match

players shall keep off the center of the rink except the playing party and his sweepers.

7 (2) Skips and vice-skips may stand within or behind the house but the skip of the playing party has priority. Behind the sweeping line the privileges of both skips shall be equal.

Rule 8 (1) Each player must play from the hack and in the delivery of the rock, the rock shall be released from the hand before any part of the rock reaches the nearest hog line. In the event of an infraction, the rock shall be removed from play.

Rule 8 (6) Each player must be ready to play when his turn comes. Should a player play an opponent's rock, the correct rock shall be put in its place.

Rule 8 (7) If a player plays out of turn:

(a) The rock may be stopped and returned to the player.

(b) If the rock completes the play and comes to rest, the missed rock shall be played by the player missing his turn as the last rock of his team for that end.

8 (8) If it cannot be decided who missed playing the rock, the lead

shall play the last rock for his team that end.

Rule 9   Sweeping shall be under the direction of the skips from the tee line to tee line, but behind the tee line or sweeping line both teams shall have equal rights with only one member of each team eligible to sweep.

Rule 10 (1)   If a running rock be affected by any member of the team to whom it belongs, it shall be removed from the ice by the playing side.

10 (2)   But if its course or position is altered by an opposing party, it shall be replaced by the skip to which it belongs.

Rule 11   All matches shall be of a certain number of ends or "by time as established at the outset. In case of a tie play shall continue until either team scores.

Rule 12   A rink shall score one point for every rock which is nearer the tee or center of the rings than any rock of the opposing rink. Any rock touching the outer circle is eligible. Disputed shots shall be determined by the acting skips or by the umpire or by a neutral party, in that order. No measuring is allowed until the end terminates except by the umpire to decide whether or not a rock is in play.

Rule 13   On appeal, the umpire or the committee responsible shall decide whether the ice is playable. If postponed, the match commences "de novo."

Analysis of the Curling Delivery

Successful performance may be displayed through a variety of forms and techniques, but it is rare when they violate established performance principles. In other words, for a given act or sequence of skills, there is a generally accepted good form, consistent with kinesiological, physical, and psychological evidence, with variations of the ideal form. This is not to deny the possibility of success in spite of form, but rather to emphasize the probability of success and form going together (Singer, 1968, p. 118).

Form provides direction for the learner and facilitates the learning of specified skills. This is not to say that there is one and only one way to execute a given task but there are basic fundamentals to which one must adhere in order to become successful. The author will attempt to outline basic fundamentals necessary to efficiently and effectively develop a sound curling delivery.

The technique of delivering a curling rock is divided into four phases: sitting position, backswing, forward swing and the follow-through. The purpose of this chapter is to describe the procedure of each phase.

SITTING POSITION

A sound curling delivery begins in the hack. The position the curler takes in the hack will have a major effect upon the rest of his delivery. The

33

curler must take a comfortable and effect "set" position in the hack, just as the sprinter must take his particular position in the starting blocks. Like the sprinter, the curler's aim is to initiate forward momentum with a minimum amount of lateral motion. The target is the skip's broom, thus the curler aims at it with his feet, knees, hips, shoulders and throwing arm. Let us now get into the sitting position.

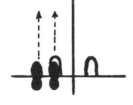

Figure 1

Approach the hack from the rear and place your feet into the position shown in Figure 1 (assuming that the curler is right-handed). Note that both feet are very close together. The reason for this is to establish a single point of balance. The advantage of a single point of balance will become more evident as we progress through the description of a smooth and effective delivery. It is most important that the feet point directly at the imaginary line of flight to the skip's broom.

If after a concerted effort you find that you are unable to get up into the backswing with balance and confidence from placing both feet together, then you might move the left foot forward as in Figure 2. This is recommended to beginners if it appears that the rock is drawing them off line, or they are losing their balance during the backswing. A word of caution must go with this foot position. Be sure that the left foot is pointing towards the skip's broom and that it has not wandered out to the left, thus taken away the single point of balance. The entire delivery relies on balance so take stock of the position of your feet now before thinking of the position of your knees, hips and shoulders. Having placed your feet correctly, you must take the sitting position as in Figure 3. As shown in the figure, you are sitting on the calves of your legs, not the heels.

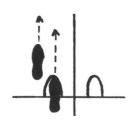

Figure 2

34

The body weight must be kept on the balls of the feet and thighs parallel to the ice surface. If you have moved your left foot forward in your sitting position, your right knee may point down toward the ice slightly. The main object is that you are in a ready or "go" position. You should feel balanced over your right foot in the hack, with head and shoulders leaning or slouched forward approximately 30 degrees from the vertical. Knees and feet should be close together, pointing directly at the skip's broom. Hips and shoulders must be squarely facing the imaginary line to the skip's broom. Most important is that you are comfortable, relaxed and in perfect balance.

Figure 3

From Figure 4 we can see what happens when you become careless and too relaxed in the sitting position. The weight has shifted from the balls of the feet to the heels. This has caused the center of gravity to shift to the hack, thus making it very awkward to get up into the backswing. Remember, be comfortable in the sitting position but keep the weight well forward so that you feel strong and ready to start the backswing phase of the delivery.

Figure 4

Having done side and overhead views let us look at the front view in the sitting position. Recall for a moment that you were asked to keep your legs together. Doing this makes it easier to check your body position in regard to Figure 5. It shows the square and blocked effect that you must try to achieve. This can be accomplished only with feet together, and thighs in a horizontal position. The shoulders must be squared to the imaginary line of flight to the skip's broom. It is imperative to recognize good posture at this stage of the delivery as it has a profound bearing on the execution of the backswing.

Figure 5

35

Figure 6

If the left foot has been moved forward to be more comfortable you must then use the right leg to sight with as the left knee will be pointing upward and distort the line formed by keeping the legs close together. Hips and shoulders still remain in a position directly facing the line of flight.

Some common faults incurred in the sitting position are sighted in the following figures.

Figure 7   Figure 8

In Figure 7 the curler has placed the rock too far forward and thus drawn his body off line. He has transfered weight to the rock and will find it difficult to move into his backswing. In Figure 8 the opposite situation has occurred, shifting the weight to the heels. He will likely shift weight to the rock in an attempt to move into the backswing. In both cases these positions will not give the curler a feeling of readiness for the backswing phase of his delivery.

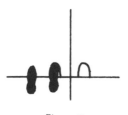

Figure 9

Figure 9 shows that the feet are too far apart, thus creating a double point of balance. This generally causes the curler to step back in his delivery, thus destroying the rhythm and ease of the pendular delivery action. Figure 10 depicts the curler who leans over to line up his shot. Avoid this procedure as you will naturally move in behind the rock in the forward delivery of the rock. It is most important that you keep your hips squarely under. A hip shift to the right can cause difficulties when you attempt to move in behind your rock in the forward phase of delivery.

Figure 10

BROOM POSITION

The curler has a large degree of freedom in regard to broom position. The following figures will give you some idea of the range of positions recommended.

Figure 11

A few points to remember in regard to broom positions are: put as little weight on the broom as possible throughout the execution of the delivery; do not allow the broom hand to go above the height of your shoulder; keep the broom arm fully extended but not rigid; keep the broom forward to maintain proper shoulder position. Pay no attention to broom position as you go into the backswing, think only of it as a counter-balance for the rock. The most satisfactory position for the broom is where it feels most comfortable and aids in maintenance of body balance. The longer the sliding delivery that the curler develops the more he will tend to bring the broom forward. Under no circumstances should the curler deliver a rock without the broom in hand; it is a necessary balancing device.

Figure 12

ROCK PLACEMENT

One of the most important features of the hack or lining up position is the placing of the rock in its proper place so that it may be taken up into the backswing on the imaginary line from the rock to the skip's broom. The following diagrams will show clearly where the rock should be placed for the in- or out-turn when delivering at a target down the middle of the sheet.

Figure 13

The backswing path of the rock must be an extension of the imaginary line of flight to the skip's broom. At no time can the rock leave this direct line of flight. Thus the position shown in Figure 14 is the correct position regardless of foot position. The rock position shown in Figure 15 will generally result in a rotational effect of the body in the backswing, which will be discussed later. Rock position of Figure 16 will generally lead to a loss of balance in the initial movement of the delivery phase.

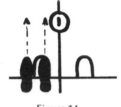

Figure 14

Figure 15

Figure 16

Figure 17

The grip, which will be covered in the next section, is firm but must leave the arm relaxed so that the rock is directly under the right shoulder as the curler pulls up into the backswing. The head-on view of Figure 17 illustrates proper rock position by the dark outline, whereas the dotted lines show improper position of the rock. A rock in the proper position can be taken into the backswing with little or no deviation from the intended line, whereas the dotted rocks will have to be corrected during the swing. It is recommended that someone stand at the hog line and check your rock position so that it will remain on the proper line of delivery when going into the backswing.

Figure 18

The rock should be placed at arm's length as demonstrated in Figure 18. The arm should be fully extended, though relaxed. At no time during the delivery should the arm bend at the elbow. It must be kept rigid throughout the entire delivery of the rock.

38

In summary, the basic points to remember when taking the sitting position are:

— feet and knees together and pointing directly toward the skip's broom.
— thighs in horizontal position, shoulders and hips directly facing the intended line of flight.
— body weight on the balls of the feet.
— broom in comfortable position.
— rock placed on intended line of flight at full arm's length.

It is often helpful to take a deep breath and release it. This serves two purposes; first, it tends to put the curler in a relaxed, slouch position (Figure 19) and, second, relieves a certain amount of stress and muscle tension.

Figure 19

THE GRIP

The grip of the rock must be one of fingertip control at all times. Under no circumstances is the curler allowed to clutch the rock. The more gentle the grip the more gentle will the release be. Figures 20 and 21 will give some idea as to the way to start to take hold of the rock. It is important that the grip should be one that will allow you to swing and deliver the rock but not one that will encourage you to manipulate or steer the rock during delivery. Your sitting position is one of comfort and relaxation, thus the grip must also be a fingertip control and free from tension. The control on the rock must stem from the forefinger and thumb, the other fingers act merely as guides. This is best accomplished by keeping the wrist well up as illustrated in Figure 22. Figure 23 shows the incorrect manner generally caused by the rock being placed too far forward, the grip being too firm, or having body

Figure 20   21

Figure 22   23

39

weight on the rock, thus causing undue manipulation of the rock in the delivery.

It is nearly impossible to deliver a curling rock in a manner such that it will travel in a predetermined straight line. Because of the nature of the rock's running surface it tends to travel in an arching path. Therefore, a deliberate spin or turn is placed on the rock upon release, thus an accurate judgment of its projected path can be made. For most consistent effect it is recommended that the rock shall make between two and one-half to three revolutions while traveling from hack to house. A spinning rock tends to curl less and a rock with fewer revolutions tends to lose its turn and thus lose its effectiveness.

Figure 24

The grip is much the same for both the in-turn and the out-turn, but the positioning of the handle generally varies slightly from one turn to the other. In positioning the rock for an in-turn (clockwise) the goose neck is pointed directly at the intended line of flight. The handle must maintain this direction throughout the delivery until the beginning of release. In positioning the rock for the out-turn (counter-clockwise) the handle is back-turned approximately 45 degrees. As in the execution of the in-turn the handle must maintain the related position throughout the delivery until commencement of the release. It is important to stress again the need for a high wirst and fingertip control throughout the delivery of the rock. Figures 24 and 25 illustrate the positions for the in-turn and out-turn, respectively.

Figure 25

THE BACKSWING

The primary function of the backswing is to provide the appropriate momentum to suc-

40

cessfully complete the forward swing and thus execute the desired shot. The backswing shall be slow, deliberate and controlled so that the curler will arrive at the top of the backswing with balance and confidence.

The two most important factors in the execution of the backswing are BALANCE and RHYTHM. After taking the sitting position the curler must focus his eyes on the skip's broom and then start to think of rhythm. When the curler is convinced in his mind that this particular rhythm is sufficient for the shot to be executed, he must try to let this flow into a feel for the shot.

Concentration and practice will build up this confidence and judgment. After this rhythm and weight have been chosen, he must think of throwing the rock with a balanced swing and follow through. The delivery must be one continuous movement with that predetermined rhythm constant throughout the entire delivery.

41

Figure 26

Figure 27

From the basic sitting position, once again illustrated in Figure 26, the backward swing phase of the delivery begins. The backswing is initiated with a rising action of the body, as illustrated by the arrows in the figure. This rising action begins with the pulling back of the rock, followed with the raising of the lower part of the back, and finally with the raising of the head and shoulders. Of course, the three actions must be totally coordinated into one series of movements. The action can best be described by a pulling back on the rock and a standing up action all in one smooth motion. As illustrated in Figure 27, the head rises and actually moves forward. This is necessary to maintain body weight on the hack foot and only the hack foot. Under no circumstances shall body weight be shifted to the left foot in the backswing. This step back action causes a breakdown in rhythm and often forces the curler to leave the predetermined line of flight. The left foot must react in unison with the rock. As the rock is taken back the left foot moves back to aid in maintenance of balance. The left foot shall move back along the ice never losing contact with it. The author suggests that the direction of the kick back be somewhat in relation to the length of slide. The longer the slide the more should the kick back deviate from the conventional 45-degree angle to straight back. If the curler wishes to develop a long slide it is recommended to take the left foot straight back. This reduces lateral action and tends to prevent a drifting effect in the follow through. The curler must be warned that he must at all times be sure not to kick back around behind his right foot as this will cause difficulties in maintaining an accurate line of direction.

The result, or position, at the top of the

backswing should be that the weight of body and rock be almost entirely on the right foot. The right knee must never lock but be bent slightly and remain pointing at the broom. The stabilization of the right knee to the intended line of flight is a major consideration for the curler in controlling his line of flight in the forward phase of the delivery. The left leg has been moved back toward the bump board, approximately 16 to 20 inches. The left arm and broom act only as counter balance for the curler and thus it is not of major importance to their movement as long as they do not draw the curler off line.

The entire execution of the backswing is one of coordination. As soon as the curler has pulled the rock back along the ice, even or parallel with his right leg, the left leg and right arm should then go back together. The left arm may or may not join in at this point. Think of rhythm during the backswing and it will not be long before you will feel balanced and compact while doing it.

Figure 28

Let us now take a look at Figure 28 which illustrates the path that the rock will travel during the back and forward swing, so that we may concentrate fully on balance and rhythm during the swing. In checking this portion of the swing the curler will need the assistance of a coach. The height of the backswing will vary with the particular rhythm but the other elements should remain constant. A critical point will be reached if the rock comes back further than 12 inches. If it occurs the point of balance will shift to the back foot and thus the smooth rhythm will be lost in the weight shift. The other portion of the diagram deals with getting the rock out in front of you during the forward swing so that the left (sliding) foot may come in behind the rock. This sliding foot MUST eventually get in behind the rock to enable you to slide down the imaginary line of flight toward the skip's broom. The 2:3 ratio would indicate that if the rock were placed 18 inches in front of the hack during the sitting position, then it would touch down to the ice during the forward swing at approximately 27 inches from the hack. At the beginning this may seem quite difficult, but as the curler practices he will find that it is a real help in the development of a slide delivery.

In summary, the basic points to remember are:

— rhythm and motion required for the shot to be made.
— pull back on the rock and get up in the delivery to create pendular momentum on the rock.
— keep the body weight directly on the right foot, stabilizing the right knee.
— keep your eyes focused on the skip's broom throughout the delivery.
— grip the rock gently and cradle it with the fingers.
— avoid turning the handle in the backswing.
— do not manipulate the rock during the delivery.

THE FORWARD SWING

In coming out of the backswing the rock must come forward in a pendular action, always in line with the skip's broom. The rock must lead the way into the forward slide. The all-important factor is that of maintaining straightforward action with no lateral motion.

As mentioned earlier, the right knee must maintain the direction toward the broom—it is the guide to a straight slide. As illustrated in Figure 29, the forward swing is initiated by the rock.

Figure 29

This is followed with a dropping of the hips and a constant pressure applied against the hack. The arm must be kept fully extended throughout the delivery. Eyes are focused on the skip's broom continuously. The left leg and right arm must be in coordinated motion as you come through so that when the rock is meeting the ice the left foot is coming in behind it. If your left foot comes forward too soon it will come in beside the rock, which is most undesirable. The same thing will occur if the curler bends his right arm in the forward motion of the delivery. If the left foot comes in too late, a balance problem may occur.

Figure 30

Figure 30 illustrates the sequence of events in the forward phase of the delivery. From the top of the backswing the pendular action of the rock initiates the forward motion; bring the hips forward and down as the head and shoulders settle into the follow through position. The right leg remains in the hack until the body is extended. As the right leg leaves the hack it should be relaxed and in a straight line with the right arm and sliding foot.

Figure 31

The most important aspect of the slide delivery comes into play at this time—that of the FLAT FOOT SLIDE. The left foot must be placed flatly on the ice and directly behind the rock with the knee tucked firmly into the left armpit. This will give considerable stability to the slide delivery.

At this point it is wise to stress the "straight line" effect of the delivery. The rock, hand, elbow, foot, trail knee, and trail foot must all be in a straight line to the intended line of flight. The entire body must be directly behind the rock in perfect line to the target at which the curler is aiming.

Figure 32

Figures 33 and 34 serve to illustrate what has been previously mentioned, that of the grip. Figure 33 illustrates the high wrist and fingertip action necessary for an effective release. Whereas Figure 34 shows that the curler is placing weight on the rock and thus will have difficulty imparting the turn onto the rock. This is often the situation when curlers attempt to use what is commonly known as a toe slide delivery.

Figure 33

With the increase of the length of slide it is common practice to allow the broom to come in contact with the ice and thus aid in balance. However, it is most important not to place any amount of weight on the broom as it will cause the curler to be drawn from the line of flight, thus making it difficult to control the direction of the rock.

Figure 34

IMPARTING THE TURN

To impart the turn onto the rock, you must put it on gradually with the use of the forefingers and thumb and the wrist only. The turn should be put on in the last three feet of contact with the rock. You must not change the direction of the rock, thus taking it from the predetermined line of flight. Thus avoid any rotation of the elbow and keep the shoulder rigid throughout the delivery. It is often helpful, especially on the out-turn, to keep the throwing elbow up and in to avoid throwing a somewhat floating rock which does not take the turn as early as the normal rock does. Also keep the wrist up high so that the release will be smooth and clean. As mentioned earlier, the turn must be put on with the forefingers and thumb, not with the little finger, as it will again cause a floating effect on the rock.

Figure 35

47

In regard to the amount of turn to be imparted, it is important to remember that the wrist should not rotate more than 45 degrees for either turn. The in-turn is started from the straight handle position and rotated through 45 degrees in a clockwise direction. The out-turn begins from a 45-degree clockwise rotation and is rotated 45 degrees counter-clockwise.

In summary the forward delivery phase balance and straight line motion are the key factors to effective and efficient execution of the shot. The forward motion must be fluid, coordinated, and without stress. Remember to get the rock well out ahead of the body, placing body in a direct line behind the rock. At all times keep your eyes on the skip's broom. The illustrations of Figure 36 show various angles of the slide delivery, accentuating the flat sliding foot, rock placement in regard to body, and the general body lay-out.

Figure 36

THE FOLLOW THROUGH

The follow through begins with a gentle release of the rock, continuously maintaining the straight forward sliding action to the broom. If you develop a follow-through position that will give you balance, control and confidence and a free release of the rock while sliding in a straight line to the broom, then the major part of your delivery will be mastered.

Figure 37 illustrates a sound follow through as an extension of the delivery of the rock. Note that the hand is held up after the release of the rock, thus making certain that the release was smooth and clean. It is at this stage that the curler might go to what is considered the toe slide. In an attempt to get down and "sight in" your shot, you might wish to tip up onto the toe just as you are in the process of release. Figure 38 illustrates the tip-over type of follow through often used. It merely serves the purpose of getting down to see how effectively one hit the predetermined target, that of the skip's broom. This type of a slide, though very effective, puts a great deal of stress and strain on the left knee, thus in many cases causing serious injury to knee ligaments.

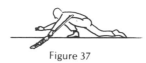

Figure 37

Figure 38

In general the follow through is simply a smooth, rhythmical continuation of the entire delivery. The main points to keep in mind are the straight line effect, getting down as low as possible behind the rock, with the rock a full arm's length directly in front of the curler.

Concentration, confidence and rhythm are the keys to success in curling. We must concentrate upon the shot to be made in regard to the type of shot, position of shot and weight necessary to best execute the shot. We must have confidence within ourselves that each and every shot can be made. In order to achieve this confidence we must start with a sound basic delivery pattern. Thus we must remember that a sound delivery is the basis upon which we can build to become a proficient shot-maker. The delivery must be smooth and rhythmical to be consistently effective. Thus from the sitting position through to the last movement in the follow through it is

essential to concentrate and execute with per-
fection in order to get the desired result.

As the curler goes into a new season of curling it
is well for him to remember the following
quotation:

> The duration of an athletic contest is only a
> few minutes, while the training for it may
> take many weeks of arduous work and
> continuous exercise of self-effort. The real
> value of sport is not the actual game played
> in the limelight of applause but the hours of
> dogged determination and self-discipline
> carried out alone, imposed and supervised
> by an exacting conscience. The applause
> soon dies away, the prize is left behind, but
> the character you build up is yours forever
> (Royal Roads Military College, Victoria,
> British Columbia).

7.
The Art of Sweeping

Experiments conducted in Switzerland as early as 1924 have been aimed at conclusive proof that sweeping creates desired effects on the movement of a curling rock. Meyer and Werlich of Galt, Ontario, have more recently conducted experiments, as has Muirhead of Medicine Hat, Alberta.

In general it is agreed that sweeping plays a major role in the game of curling. Research shows that pebble on the ice surface is the most important factor to effective sweeping. Sweeping causes a melting effect on the pebble and thus temporarily creates a film of moisture which reduces friction on the surface. Therefore, a vigorous and powerful sweeping action is essential to cut into the pebble and create this effect. It is also theorized that the vigorous sweeping action immediately in front of the rock cuts the air currents, creating a partial vacuum thus reducing air resistance on the rock. Of course, the most obvious reason for brandishing the broom is to remove debris from the path of the curling rock.

The foregoing reasons for sweeping preclude that sweeping must be vigorous in order to be effective. The main ingredients to effect sweeping are power and rhythm. It is the person, not the broom, which determines effectiveness of sweeping. Thus sweeping is an art which can and must be mastered by ladies and men alike.

The first consideration is that of the broom. The curler should select a broom to conform to his or her strength and ability to sweep with it. Most brooms are made in light, medium and heavy sizes. It is important to realize that a broom must go through a breaking in period. This generally means one or two games before the broom feels comfortable. The weight of the broom should be such that the broom works for you in making it "snap." In turn you must be careful not to get a broom too light for you as it will not have enough recoil to allow you to take fast, rhythmical strokes.

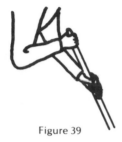

Figure 39

Our next concern is the grip for sweeping. As illustrated in Figures 39 and 40, the upper hand is placed firmly at the top of the handle while the lower hand is placed approximately half way up the handle. Two basic grips are used for the lower hand. Figure 39 illustrates the overhand grip, which is generally considered the most effective. This grip puts excessive strain on the wrist and thus takes a great deal of practice to execute effectively. The underhand grip as designated in Figure 40 creates much less strain but reduces the power of the sweeping stroke slightly.

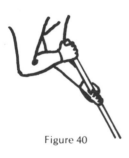

Figure 40

At this point the lower elbow must be brought in underneath you as you sweep. The broom should be held at approximately a 30-degree angle to the vertical position to utilize the entire effect of the sweeping stroke. The stroke should also be perpendicular to the path of the rock.

The stroke itself must be produced by the upper hand with the lower hand acting as the fulcrum. Power is applied by the upper hand, forcing the broom firmly onto the ice. With the nylon synthetic brooms it has become necessary to apply some power and even some movement with the lower hand in order to maintain speed, rhythm and yet power. The basic sweeping action must be that of applying force on your forward stroke rather than the backward motion. With practice the backward stroke is strengthened by wrist action of the lower hand. The concentration on the forward action will aid greatly in the development of rhythm and thus effectiveness.

To determine the side from which you should sweep, just follow this simple rule: If you place your right hand on the lower part of the broom handle you should sweep from the right side of the rock; if your left hand is down, sweep from the left. If this rule is followed you will always face the direction of the path of the rock.

Footwork in sweeping is of vital importance. It must be such that it does not detract from the rhythm previously created. One of the most effective techniques is that of sliding on the lead foot and pushing or driving with the other. The knees should be slightly flexed and body leaning well over the rock. The sweeper will be in position to glance forward to be aware of what is in front of him and the distance left to go. This shuffle-slide step will aid in the development of rhythm and effective and efficient sweeping power.

Probably the most effective way of improving team sweeping is to develop rhythmical sweeping in unison with one another. In order to develop this action, the person nearest the rock must establish the beat and the other sweeper then falls in with him. This togetherness in sweeping is a great psychological uplift in that it makes sweeping seem easier and more beneficial.

Sweeping is a great help to shot making, but one

must know when to sweep. Basically either the lead or second member of the team should become the judge for all draw shots. The skip must still call the sweep in terms of line of flight of the shot. Every shot should be gently brushed to maintain a clean surface for the rock. Generally speaking the effectiveness of hit and roll shots are determined by the accurate and precise judgment of the sweepers rather than the person delivering the rock. Well trained sweepers play a major role in the outcome of a game.

The Training Program

Strength, endurance and flexibility are the three major concerns in the development of a curler. Besides developing a high level of general fitness, the curler must work on specific conditioning and flexibility exercises. The curler must develop leg and back strength, with extra stress on strengthening knees and lower back muscles. The flexibility of hips, knees and back are of prime importance to the delivery phase of the curler. Endurance is required so that the curler can sweep effectively for 10 ends and continue to deliver his rocks efficiently.

To increase the strength of a muscle it must be subjected to a load greater than that to which it is normally accustomed. Thus weight training is recommended. In general, exercises should be done in sets of 10 repetitions per exercise. Thus the weights to be used are determined by the athlete's ability to execute six to 10 repetitions of a particular exercise. If six repetitions in succession cannot be done, the weight is too heavy and should be reduced. If more than 10 repetitions can readily be done, the weight is too light and thus more should be added. Once you can comfortably execute 10 repetitions of each exercise described below, the weights should again be increased. Exercises of this type should be done three days a week, with a day of rest between lifting days.

To further improve endurance a "continuous training program", including distance running, jogging, stair climbing, maximum pushups, sit-ups, leg raises, etc., must be developed.

55

The following basic weight training program is most readily adaptable to both male and female alike.

GROUP 1
(USE ¼ OF YOUR BODY WEIGHT)

Exercise 1. Curls.

Figure 41

Curls are done to increase the strength of the biceps, triceps and forearms. Be sure that the back is held upright and rigid throughout the exercise.

Exercise 2. Bent-over rowing.

Figure 42

Bent-over rowing is done to develop the upper and lower back muscles as well as the arms and wrists. The back must be kept in a horizontal position while the arms do the actual rowing exercise.

Exercise 3. Press behind the neck.

Figure 43

Pressing is done for the development of upper back, shoulders and triceps. Feet are placed shoulder width apart, back straight and eyes looking straight ahead.

Exercise 4. Sit-ups.

Figure 44

Sit-ups with weights are done to strengthen abdominal muscles. Use approximately 10 pounds of weights behind the head. Have a partner hold your feet down or hook them underneath a bar. Maintain a bent knee position throughout the exercise.

GROUP II
(USE ⅓ OF YOUR BODY WEIGHT)

Exercise 5. Lateral Raises.

Figure 45

The lateral raises will help to develop the abdominal muscles, upper and lower back and

56

shoulders. In doing this exercise it is important to bring the weights up to equal height at the same time.

Exercise 6. High Pulls.

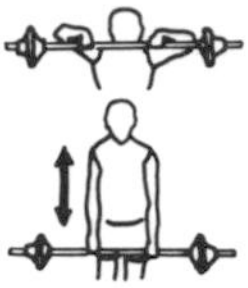

Figure 46

High pulls help to develop abdominals, back, shoulders, arms and wrists. The weights must be pulled up to nose level, with the wrists held above the bar as illustrated in Figure 46. As in the lateral raises, be sure to bring the bar up evenly with right and left arm.

Exercise 7. Back-Lying Leg Raises

This exercise develops the thigh and the abdominal muscles. Use seven pounds of weight and build up to 20 pounds. Raise the legs six inches from the floor, hold and lower just to touch the floor, then raise and repeat the exercise for 10 repetitions.

Figure 47

GROUP III
(USE ½ OF YOUR BODY WEIGHT)

Exercise 8. Front squats.

Front squats are primarily done to develop thigh and calf muscles. With feet shoulder-width apart, maintain weights as illustrated in Figure 48. Do squats so that the thighs and calves make a 90-degree angle with one another.

Figure 48

Exercise 9. Straddle (Geofferson) Lift.

The straddle lift is another leg strengthener. The back must remain in an upright position throughout the exercise. Squat down far enough to touch the weights to the floor, and repeat.

Figure 49

Exercise 10. Cheating Press.

This is an overall body development exercise. The weights are placed on the shoulders, the athlete does a partial squat and then pushes the weights up to arm's length above the head with the use of the legs and arms at the same time.

Figure 50

A sound weight training program can become a most rewarding experience for the athlete. The author has found that through a comprehensive weight training program the teaching of the fundamentals of the curling delivery has become easier and more precise, in that the athlete has the strength and coordination to execute the movements with much greater ease and efficiency. The use of weights and isometrics has become most essential in all sports, curling being no exception.

The use of warm-up activities prior to athletic contests goes back to the days of the early Egyptians. They used the technique of warming up prior to bodily contact during games. Warming up as a safeguard to avoid muscular injury has long been an accepted fact. Although there is considerable agreement among researchers that there are physiological benefits from warm-up there is much controversy as to the type of warm-ups most valuable and indeed if warm-up in fact enhances the performance level of the athlete in a specified motor skill. In the game of curling it is the author's contention that a warm-up is beneficial as a safeguard against injury because of the 40-pound rock used in the activity, and that the warm-up activity tends to reduce muscle tension and strain, thus the athlete will be more relaxed. Relaxation is conducive to improved performance.

The following exercises may serve for both conditioning exercises and warm-up exercises. The author most highly recommends the following for warm-ups just prior to competition.

Exercise 1. Push-ups.

The athlete lies on the stomach, hands under the

shoulders, pushes the body upward, keeping it rigid. This is an excellent exercise for the development of arms and back to add power to sweeping and control in delivery of the curling rock.

Exercise 2. Sit-ups.

From a back-lying prone position with hands behind the head, lift up into a sitting position, return and repeat. This exercise is an abdominal and lower back conditioner and a good flexibility exercise.

Exercise 3. Alternate Leg Thrusts.

The body is in a prone position on hands and toes. Alternately thrust knees forward, bringing the foot well underneath the chest. Do the exercise rhythmically, bouncing from one foot to the other, thus developing flexibility of the hips to better get into the slide position described earlier. This is one of the finest flexibility and knee, conditioning exercises applicable to curling.

Figure 51

Exercise 4. Alternate Knee Bends.

Place the hands on the right knee, then maintaining an upright position as illustrated in Figure 52, move the body weight over the right knee and bounce three times, shift to a similar position over the left knee and repeat as before. This exercise again helps to develop and strengthen the knee. It is essential that much effort is made to strengthen knee ligaments as there is a great deal of stress on them in the execution of the delivery of the curling rock.

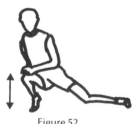

Figure 52

Outlined above are a few exercises to increase flexibility, strength and endurance—there are many more which can and should be utilized. It is most important that we do comprehensive conditioning and basic exercises to warm up prior to beginning competition on the ice.

59

9.
The Practice Session

One of the greatest weaknesses in the development of the curler today is that of meaningless practices. The fundamentals of curling, as outlined in previous pages of this book, lie in the delivery of the curling rock. Therefore, to make curling practice meaningful and profitable, the curler must have a basic practice plan with drills to accentuate specific fundamentals as described in the instructional phase of this book.

For the novice a great deal of time must be spent on the delivery in the early stages of training. A general practice should start with loosening up exercises, followed by some free sliding down the length of the ice. The free slide exercise refers to taking three steps and dropping down into the slide delivery position and sliding, then standing up, taking three more steps and continuing the sliding drill.

Drills which have proved most effective in the development of the slide delivery are described below.

THE FREE SLIDE DRILL

This drill is used mainly for the long slide deliveries to improve balance and poise. Stand one stride behind the hack, step into the hack with your right foot, push out, dropping your hips quickly but smoothly thus falling into your slide delivery, and slide toward a target. As the curler gains confidence, he should increase the speed at which he approaches the hack and thus slide 40 to 50 feet down the ice.

This long slide gives him a long time to check his sliding technique and position of hands, knees, shoulders, trail leg, etc. This drill is excellent for the development of confidence in the slide, balance and a stright slide.

THE FREE SLIDE TARGET DRILL

A target is placed on the near hog line. The curler takes the proper sitting position in the hack, lines up in order to hit the target. Without the use of the rock, he slides out directly on target.

BARRIER DRILL

To combat the problem of tailing around with the trail leg this drill becomes most helpful. Place six rocks out on the ice as illustrated in Figure 53. The pairs of rocks should be approximately 18 inches apart. Execute the running Free Slide and the normal delivery of the curling rock through the barriers. The barriers will help to make the curler aware of his body position, specifically the trail leg. The distance between the rocks may be reduced as the curler gains greater confidence.

Figure 53

BROOM DRILL

Have a person hold a broom at various positions along the near hog line, take the proper position in the hack, concentrating upon lining up directly facing the target. The aim is to concentrate on the line of flight toward the broom, as you must make a hack directional adjustment each time the broom changes position. Gradually have the broom moved further and further down the ice. Use both in-turns and out-turns in execution of the drill.

61

BUNCHING DRILL

Throw five rocks to the same spot with the same turn and using the same amount of ice, thus adjusting to try to bunch the rocks in definite areas in the house. This drill is especially useful for establishing consistent weights. Another variation of this drill is to throw take-out weight, thus again concentrating on one consistent take-out weight.

THE POINTS GAME

This game was actually devised to create individual competitions, but may also become a useful drill to improve shot-making. Each player takes two in-turn shots and two out-turn shots at each of nine predetermined house situations. Each successful shot counts one or two points. No rock shall be considered outside a circle unless it is entirely clear of that circle.

The ice surface shall be marked off as illustrated in Figure 54.

Areas 1 and 2 are 10 feet from the center of the house.

Areas 3 and 4 are two feet from the center line and parallel to areas 1 and 2.

Area 5 is eight feet from the center of the house.

Areas 6 and 7 are 12 feet from the center of the house and at 45-degree angles of the sweeping line.

Areas 8 and 9 are two feet six inches from the center of the house and at 45-degree angles of the sweeping line.

Areas 10 and 12 are two feet from the center of the house.

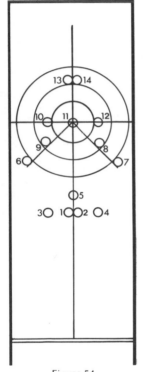

Figure 54

62

Area 11 is in the center of the house, or on the button.

Areas 13 and 14 are four feet from the center of the house.

Placed rocks are designated by ● , played rocks are designated by ○

1. Striking

A rock is placed in area number 12. If struck, count 1 point; if struck out of the 12-foot circle, count 2.

2. Inwicking

Rocks are placed in areas 8 and 11. If the played rock strikes the number 8 rock on the inside, score 1 point; if it strikes both, score 2 points.

3. Drawing

Draw for the house, if the rock stops in 12-foot circle, score 1 point; if it stops within the 8-foot circle, score 2 points.

4. Guarding

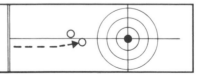

A rock is placed in area 11. The guard must cross the hog line and not touch the placed rock. If it is within six inches of the tee line, count 1 point, if it touches the tee line, count 2 points.

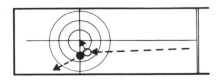

5. Chip and Lie

A rock is placed in area 12. If the rock is struck out of the 12-foot circle and the played rock rests within the 8-foot circle, count 2 points; if the played rock stops in the 12-foot circle, count 1 point.

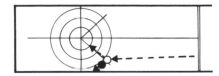

6. Wick and Roll

A rock is placed in area 7. If the rock is struck and the played rock rests in the 12-foot circle, count 1 point; if the played rock rolls to within the 8-foot cricle, score 2 points.

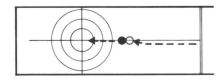

7. Raising

A rock is placed in area 5. If the played rock strikes and raises the placed rock into the 12-foot circle, count 1 point; if it is raised within the 8-foot circle, count 2 points.

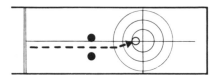

8. Drawing through a Port

Rocks are placed in areas 1 and 4. If the
played rock passes between the two
placed rocks and comes to rest in the 12-
foot circle, count 1 point; if it stops within
the 8-foot circle,count 2 points.

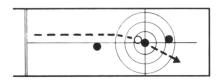

9. Chipping the Winner

Rocks are placed in areas 2, 11, and 13. If
the played rock strikes the rock in area 13,
count 1 point; if it strikes the rock in area
11, count 2 points.

The primary purpose of practice is to do things
which are meaningful and basic to the
development of fundamental skills of the activity. Thus it is hoped that the drills described
will lead to the development of more drills and
exercises to promote excellence in the game of
curling.

10.
The Scoreboard

INDIVIDUAL SCORING

The four-point scoring system has become popular to evaluate individual curlers. They compare to golfers' score cards giving the result of each shot, but say nothing of what really happened in the execution of the shot. This type of scoring is quite ample for the news media and arm-chair curlers. For the coach this card has little to offer.

In order to get a shot-by-shot analysis of the game, the four-point scoring system must be modified. The author's version of this modification is described in the following pages. Figure 55 illustrates the scoring card presently used by scoring enthusiasts.

NAME	1	2	3	4	5	6	7	8	9	10	11	12	13	TOTAL	%PTS.
LEAD															
2ND															
3RD															
SKIP															
LEAD															
2ND															
3RD															
SKIP															

Figure 55

Figure 56 illustrates a card the author has utilized as a coaching aid.

The difference between the cards is the addition of the three small boxes at the top of each block of the score card. The first box is used to record a

66

INDIVIDUAL SCORE CARD											Codes		"O" – out-turn, "I" – in-turn. "T" – take-out, "D" – draw. "W" – wide, "N" – narrow, "L" – light, "H" – heavy.		
Name	1	2	3	4	5	6	7	8	9	10	11	12	13	Tot.	% pts
Lead	I O/O H 4 4														
2nd	I D/L I O 2 4														
3rd	I T/N I T 0 4														
Skip	I T/W I T 0 4														
Lead	I T/I T N 4 0														
2nd	I T/W I D 2 4														
3rd	O D/I D 4 4														
Skip	O D/N I T L U 0 0														

Figure 56

"O" or an "I" to indicate the use of the out-turn
or the in-turn. The second box will have a "T" or
"D" recorded in it to specify a take-out shot or
draw shot. The third box is reserved for the
purpose of recording a "W," "N," "L," or "H"
indicating wide, narrow of the broom, light or
heavy in the execution of the shot. If the shot was
perfectly executed the box remains empty.

An innovation which has proven useful in attempting to overcome skip's error in reading ice
is the technique of using O's, 2's and 4's in
scoring shots when in fact the skip called the shot
correctly. Use 1's and 3's to indicate that the rock
was thrown as called for, but the skip misread the
ice. At the end of the game the card then con-
tains a record of the skip's calling errors by the
odd numbers used on the card. For example the
skip may have consistently given too much ice
for the "come around" shots.

SCORING THE DRAW SHOT

It is relatively easy to score these shots when no
other rocks are in play. If a shot has been called
for the house in front of the T line, the shot
maker has a fair bit of leeway in order to score

67

the full four points. If the shot slides behind the T line thus allowing the opposition to attempt to freeze, two points are recorded. In turn, if the shot stops short of the house no points are given. If rocks are in play in front of the house and the call is to draw for shot rock at a particular spot, for example behind a guard, drawing for second shot behind the guard would represent a two-point shot. If the shot maker were wide of the skip's broom and thus drew for shot rock but did not lie behind the guard, again two points would be recorded. If the skip makes an error in ice reading and the shot maker executes correctly and accurately, thus getting shot rock but unguarded, three points would be scored. If wrong ice were given and the shot maker drew for second shot or wicked the guard one point would be awarded, indicating a missed shot because of the skip's error.

SCORING TAKE-OUT SHOTS

In removing rocks from the front of the house, assuming the skip is reading the ice properly, a miss or a direct hit without roll is a zero shot. A hit and roll out of the playing area represents a four-point shot. A hit and roll to open the area to the eight-foot circle means two points. Subjective judgment plays a part in scoring in regard to the amount of roll satisfactory to open the front of the house. For example if your team has last rock it will suffice to keep the eight foot open, but if the opposition has last rock in the end, a rock anywhere in front of the house becomes a threat as a potential guard.

In regard to double take-out shots, you are generally awarded four points if you make the double kill but roll out as well. On the chip shot full points are awarded even when you roll out after the chip has been successfully executed. In the case of the intentional blank end a roll out is scored as four points, whereas a hit and stay might be awarded two points. Another variable to consider in the scoring of roll outs is that of effective and timely sweeping. So it becomes more and more evident that the actual scoring is not nearly as important as the statistics for further skill development and improvement.

SCORING GUARDS

There are two basic considerations. The first is that of simply wanting a rock in front of the house. In this case it is a four-point shot if it stops anywhere between the hog line and the house within a reasonable range of where it was called for. Two points are given if it comes to rest in the house and in front of the T line. No points can be given for a guard which ultimately stops behind the T line, as this could well force your skip into a hitting game when in fact he is trying to set up a situation to steal a point.

SCORING FREEZES

A freeze is a difficult shot to make and is generally called for only in delicate situations. Therefore, it is most important that it be made. Thus in scoring the freeze shot, the scorer must insist upon a nearly perfect shot for the full four points. If the shot is short but in the house two points may be awarded as is the case if the opposition rock is driven back but not through the house, because the opposition might drive your rock back onto their own rock in an attempt to remove it.

At the end of the game a summary sheet is prepared for each curler and the following practice is then geared to the improvement of individual difficulties. Thus it can be readily seen that the score card is an effective coaching aid for coach and curler. Scoring has long been a subject of controversy, as often percentages do not reflect the actual outcome of the game. The game is determined by the score on the official scoreboard, thus percentages on the individual score card are secondary to the curler and the coach. Too often curlers become overconscious of the individual percentages, thus it is important that the individual scoring card is used primarily as a teaching aid rather than a set of statistics for losers.

In summary, no points indicate a complete miss by the shot-maker; one point indicates a complete miss because of the skip's error in reading ice; two points represent a half shot (such as a roll out); three points indicate a half shot made with the skip's error, four points represent a perfectly executed shot. In the case of a fluke no points can be awarded regardless of the results.

No scoring system is infallible. The player is bound to be penalized in situations where he is not at fault. The foregoing system has simply been an attempt to efficiently and effectively give the coach and curler a shot-by-shot overview of his performance. Whatever system is employed, scoring for improvement of skills is essential.

TEAM SCORING

The object of the game of curling is to complete each end with as many rocks as possible nearer

the center of the circles than the nearest opposition rock. If team A and team B were playing
one another, the team scoring on any particular
end would be determined by the rock nearest the
center of the circle. One point is scored for each
rock nearer the center of the circles than the
nearest opposition rock. If team A has a rock in
the four-foot circle and team B has any number
of rocks in the 12-foot or eight-foot circles, the
team A rock nullifies all opposing rocks farther
from the center. Therefore, if team B has last
rock in the end and thereby uses it to remove the
opposition rock, all team B rocks become
counting rocks.

Any rock barely biting the outer edge of the 12-
foot ring is considered a potential counting rock.
To determine whether a rock is biting the house
or which opposing rocks are nearer the center of
the house, an official measuring device is used,
taking a measure from the center of the rings to
the innermost edge of the rocks being measured.

To describe the use of the official scoreboard,
the author shall refer to Figure 57.

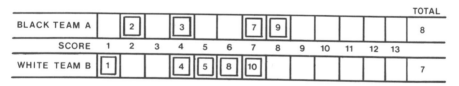

																	TOTAL
BLACK TEAM A			2			3					7		9								8
SCORE	1		2		3		4		5		6		7		8		9		10		11		12		13		
WHITE TEAM B	1					4		5		8		10									7

Figure 57

On the curling scoreboard, the middle row of
numbers refers to the score only. The upper and
lower rows refer to the ends played. Therefore, in
the first end of play team B, throwing white
handled rocks, scored one point. In end number
two, team A, throwing black handled rocks,
scored one point. On the third end team A stole
two points. To steal points means to score points

when the opposing team has the advantage of last rock in that end. In the fourth, team B scored three points tying the score at 4-4. After five complete ends of play the score was 5-4 in favor of team B.

The sixth end is not recorded on the scoreboard, thus indicating that neither team scored. When a blank end such as this occurs, the team having had last rock on the previous end retains last rock advantage in the following end. In this case it proved truly advantageous as team A scored three points on the seventh end. The eighth, ninth and tenth ends were all single point ends, with team A winning the game by a score of 8-7.

The official scoreboard indicates at a glance the overall score as well as end by end results.

11.
Game Strategy in Curling

Curling is a team sport where it is essential that each player has designated responsibilities. Too often one feels that only the skip and the third really have an effect on the outcome of the game. In order to create a team effort, each player must play an important role other than merely his or her rock delivery.

In setting out individual roles the author would suggest that one must look to the lead or second as a weight judge. He then becomes fully responsible for sweeping judgment on each rock delivered by his team members. It is much easier to make correct judgments while moving along with the rock than for the skip to make this judgment from the far end of the sheet of ice. Thus the skip is now able to concentrate upon direction of the rock and anticipate effective results. It remains the skip's prerogative to overrule when the rock approaches the nearest hog-line. Thus there are now two people very directly involved in the determination of whether a rock will reach the desired destination.

Assuming that the second man has been chosen to be the weight judge for the team, the lead man then becomes responsible for the house-cleaning chores, such as getting the rocks lined up and putting them out for each of his team members as they take their positions in the hack. This certainly helps to speed up the game and allows the throwing member of the team to concentrate mainly on his shot. It also has the added effect of having everyone responsible for particular aspects of the game.

The third man or vice skip must play the role of a backseat driver. He must become aware of ice conditions, skipping strategy of both teams and have a general overview of every situation. He is the person who must be able to help the skip out in case of a lapse of memory, or suggest alternatives in case if situations which might seriously affect the outcome of the end. It is important that the vice skip does not become domineering nor so recessive that he is of no value to the skip. It is the role of the vice skip to suggest alternatives and then have the skip make the final decision.

The skip is the field general; he must be in complete control of the situation. It is most important that he be decisive, confident and has the ability to read ice conditions and remember them from the beginning to the end of the game.

The art of ice reading is learned mainly through experience of skipping, though much can be accomplished by observing two highly competitive teams in action. Generally speaking, the ice will be somewhat heavier at the beginning of a game. This is caused by the pebble freshly applied. As the pebble wears down through the effects of sweeping and the rocks passing over it, the surface becomes keen, thus causing the rocks to move more easily over it. Rocks tend to run fairly straight in early ends; as the ice becomes keener, the rocks take more curl. Falls or slight imperfections in the surface of the ice become more obvious as the game progresses. The sharpness of the cup of the rock has a great effect upon the amount of curl produced on the rock.

The foregoing all lead to the fact that the skip

must be observant and alert to all situations and conditions before him.

The opening ends of a game are most crucial. The skip must make mental notes of each slight imperfection in the ice surface. Thus it is of utmost importance that he oberve both his team members' rocks and those of the opposition. He must observe the behaviour of the rock in terms of amount of curl and speed. It is imperative that he use the lead and second rocks to experiment on different parts of the ice, so that a complete mental picture of the conditions of the ice surface is formed. A constant lookout for changes is necessary as the ice will readily change from end to end. These changes may be caused by a change in rink temperature, humidity factors, artificial ice plant operation or various other factors.

In order to make precision judgments in regard to amount of ice necessary to execute a shot, it is essential to know exactly the amount of weight or speed a rock will have. Thus it is important that all team members throw the same amount of weight for specified shots. Basically four weights are necessary: guard weight is when the rock comes to rest approximately six feet in front of the house; draw weight is when the rock stops at the tee line; back-ring or tap-out weight is such that the rock will gently move an opposition rock to the back of the house; lastly, take-out weight will move an opposition rock to the back boards and cause it to rebound approximately two feet. Very rarely is it necessary to deliver a rock with greater velocity than normal take-out weight.

The fact that a curling game rarely presents two situations which are exactly alike makes it one of the most intriguing and challenging sports. For this reason the author shall endeavour to discuss only basic skipping strategy. From these basic skipping techniques it is up to the skip to develop an imaginative, yet realistic approach to guiding his or her team to victory.

In the following discussion please note that all diagrams on the lefthand side of the page refer to situations when the white team has advantage of last rock. The diagrams on the right side of the page refer to the opposing black team having last rock advantage.

THE FIRST END OF PLAY

This is an end of experiment and discovery. The skip should have his team use both turns. Attempt to draw to the house regardless of last rock advantage. Avoid guards and all take-outs with strong normal take-out weight. Beware of the ice running straight. Make mental notes of each shot in regard to weight and amount of curl.

**POSITIONING OF FIRST
ROCKS IN THE EARLY ENDS**

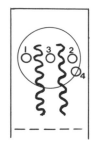

Figure 58

The aim with last rock advantage is to score at least two points. Thus one must attempt to place one's rocks in the house, spreading them well to avoid the opportunity for double take-outs. Always leave channels for the opposition to pass through. Avoid guards, as they will only serve to have the opposition roll or draw behind and thus deprive one of the opportunity to score.

Figure 59

If the opposing lead tends to draw to rocks placed on the 12-foot circle, simply draw the next rock nearer the centre of the house to force him to attempt the take-out shot.

Without having last rock advantage, the aim becomes one of forcing the opposition to score one point or to steal a point. This is often accomplished by placing a rock three feet in front of the house, anticipating a miss or a direct hit; thus having the opportunity to draw in behind for shot rock. If the opposition's hitting game is weak, simply interchange the order of the two shots. The disadvantage of this move is that if the opposition executes the take-out shot, the front-end game strategy is lost.

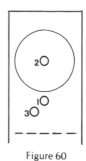

Figure 60

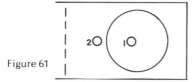

Figure 61

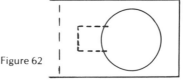

Figure 62

The area directly in front of the house must always be kept open, so that one might take advantage of the last rock to score.

In contrast, when one does not have last rock advantage, an attempt is made to seal off the front of the house to make it difficult for the opposition to score and provide an opportunity to steal a point .

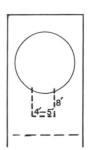

Figure 63

PLAYING GUARDS

With last rock advantage avoid playing of guards entirely. Keep a path to the four-foot circle open at all times, removing opposition guards in order to do so. If indeed a situation arises where a guard might be an advantage, it must be played close to the house.

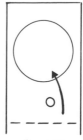

Figure 64

The situation in Figure 64 allows two alternatives: a) one might draw behind the guard. If so, one should do so around the right side; thus if the

77

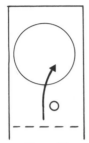

Figure 65

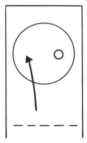

Figure 66

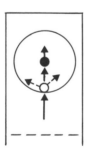

Figure 67

rock remains partially unguarded, play on the rock will cause the opposition to roll to the outside and take the play away from the center of the house. This leaves more room for error on the part of the skip with his last rock; b) remove the guard. Under no circumstances should an attempt be made to draw to the open side of the house, as it only allows the opposition an opportunity to hit and roll behind the guard.

Without last rock advantage, avoid any removal of guards. Draw around the guard toward the middle of the house, forcing the play to the four-foot ring.

If one is lying shot rock as in Figure 66, often a draw to the other side of the house is as fine an alternative as the guard, causing the opposition skip to hit and stay or draw against two potential points. Remember, a strong offense is often the most effective defense.

A frequent situation in curling is one shown in Figure 67. Often the white, in eager anticipation of removing black from scoring position, attempts a take-out, when indeed the call might well be a back ring tap-back. If the player executes it, he will be lying two, if he fails, he will in all likelihood chip his own and split the two white rocks to make second and third shot. Now the opposition must either hit with a possibility of rolling out, thus creating a potential for scoring two points, or guard leaving a situation which may result in three points.

If white does not have last rock advantage, he might attempt a draw around and freeze. If indeed he falls short of shot rock, he has made it very difficult for the opposition to score more

78

than one point. If the shot is executed perfectly, it sets up an excellent chance to steal a point.

A general rule to follow is to either draw around the guard or remove it, never draw away from it. Today's style of curling is one of strategy and finesse; the straightforward, open-hitting game is no longer effective. This is due to the fact that competitive teams have become precision-like in the execution of the draw shot, thus making it extremely difficult to score consistently using the knockout game exclusively.

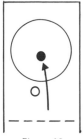

Figure 68

USING POCKETS

Whether one has last rock advantage or not, it can be advantageous to make use of opposition rocks toward the back of the house. The technique of freezing a rock to an opposition rock or placing it directly in front of an op- position rock again places a great deal of pressure on the opposition, thus stopping them from simply having to make a routine take-out shot. The use of this technique is most effective when and if a number of rocks form a cluster behind the tee-line.

It is dangerous to use this technique of freezing in the four-foot circle when one has last rock advantage, as the best counter-attack for the opposition is to turn to the same technique; thus it becomes very difficult to score large ends. In fact, the possibility of putting oneself in an impossible position with last rock to be thrown is great.

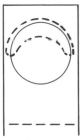

Figure 69

Generally speaking, the freeze game is utilized as a means to put additional pressure on the op- posing team, wait for a mistake, then capitalize with a big end score. Of course, the reverse may readily occur; thus the freeze technique is most generally used when a team is well behind on the scoreboard or is facing defeat in the latter ends of the game.

ACTUAL GAME SITUATIONS

In general, while the score between teams is within one or two points, the game usually follows a standard pattern. The team with last rock advantage concentrates upon placing rocks in the house, leaving them spread well apart. Guards covering the path to the middle of the house are removed. All opposition rocks are played out of the middle of the house. The team without last rock advantage attempts to place guards out front and near the center line and then draw around a guard to come to rest in the four-foot circle. This affords an excellent opportunity to score a point. All opposition rocks are removed so that the last rock advantage will be nullified.

If indeed both teams are effective until the latter part of the game, alternative strategy might be employed to outwit the opposition.

LAST END — TIE GAME

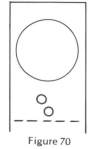

Figure 70

With last rock advantage it is most obvious that, if one removes all opposition rocks, the last rock may be used to assure victory. Thus the strategy is to simply play the hitting game.

If one is on the opposing team, the skip must deliberately place rocks in front of the house with anticipation of the opposition missing or hitting and staying out front with their rock. It is imperative that the skip attempt to get at least two rocks out front of the house. Too often he is anxious to get a rock into the house early; this simply forces the play into the house, and one mistake might well destroy a potential possibility to win. The play into the house should not occur until the third man's rocks. Thus, with two rocks out front, it provides an excellent opportunity to draw around the guards. If the opposition removes a guard, it is relatively simple to replace it. If in turn, there were only one guard, the job of adequately replacing it becomes much more difficult.

If the opposition continue to remove the guards, leaving only one, then it is advisable to draw around it with the skip's first rock. If indeed no guards are left when the skip is to throw his final rock, he must simply place it in a position which might cause the opposition to miss it. For example, there may be a slight run in the ice at a spot, or one might find that the opposing skip has had difficulty making a shot at a particular spot. Thus it is important to constantly assess the opposition and to continuously reassess ice conditions.

In a situation as in Figure 71 the rock out front of the house is much more dangerous than the rock in the house. Thus it is imperative to remove the guard rock. If the skip chose to play on the rock at the side, the opposition immediately have an opportunity to force the game to the middle and thus set up a possibility to steal the winning point. Whereas, if the front of the house remains open, that last rock advantage affords the chance to simply draw or play a straightforward take-out, without concern for guards.

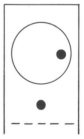

Figure 71

81

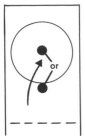

Figure 72

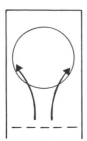

Figure 73

Figure 72 demonstrates a situation where the white team must draw in either case. If the end is down to skip rocks, the white skip must draw around the guard or, if the rock is in the house, attempt a freeze shot.

LAST END — ONE DOWN

In this situation the white team simply plays to both sides of the house, awaiting a mistake by the black team; thus setting up a situation to score two points to win. If this mistake is not forthcoming, the skip plays his last rock to tie the game and go to an extra end of play.

If the opposition get a rock into the house within the 12- or eight-foot circles, a freeze may well put additional pressure on the opposition to cause a mistake which allows for a draw to the other side of the house for a count or two.

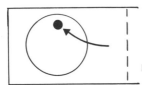

Figure 74

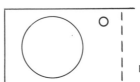

Figure 75

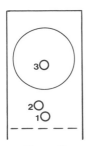

Figure 76

In this situation it may be advantageous to play a rock short of the house, thus creating cover for a second draw to the house. If the opposition should hit the guard, it would set up the draw to the other side of the house for a potential pair of points to win.

If one is one down without the advantage of last rock, the situation becomes similar to being tied playing the last end. Make certain of the tying point before trying to steal the winning point as well.

LAST END — ONE UP

With last rock advantage, one simply plays a hitting game, trying to remove all opposition rocks as well as one's own. Thus the last rock should be a simple take-out with the added bonus of not having to stay in the house to count for a win.

With the situation of "last end — one up" without last rock advantage, one is faced with the most difficult situation in curling. Three options might be considered: 1. Play a hitting game, thus playing for a tie game and attaining last rock advantage in the extra end. 2. Play a front-end game, attempting to steal a point, thus ending the game (this is rather risky). Or, 3. Play a combination of both, protecting against the possibility of giving away two points, but in turn attempting to steal a point if the opportunity presents itself.

In order to execute the third option effectively, it is important to place any guards close to, or even in the 12-foot circle, making it extremely difficult for the opposition to draw around and attain coverage from it. The important thing to remember is to constantly guard against the possibility of giving up two points.

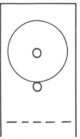

Figure 77

LAST END — TWO OR MORE DOWN

Play rocks to extreme edges, thus hopefully drawing a miss from the opposition. The second option commonly used is to place a rock midway between house and hog line near the side boards. Thus, if the opposition choose to play it off to maintain the open house concept, they must hit it on the outside edge to roll out of play or hit it

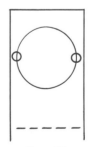

Figure 78

83

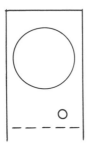

Figure 79

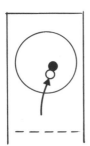

Figure 80

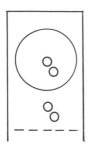

Figure 81

extremely thin on the inside to have the same result. Thus the target is reduced in size. If the opposition rock does not roll out of play, a shelter or guard is established, affording an opportunity to draw behind and applying pressure to the opposition.

If the opposition place a rock anywhere in the house, one must freeze to it and await a mistake by the opposition. The moment this comes about, the rocks must be placed well apart to avoid an opportunity for a double take-out.

Without last rock, it is essential to establish a front-end game, then go behind the guards. The aim is to draw the opposition into a draw game and then out-maneuver them.

BLANK ENDS

The purpose of the game is to outscore the opposing team. It is therefore evident that last rock advantage in an end gives a team the opportunity to capitalize on the opponents' errors and score effectively.

Thus it is good strategy to deliberately attempt to blank an end (hit and roll-out or throw a rock through the house) when one does not have an opportunity to score more than one point. This technique is most effective in later ends in order to obtain last rock advantage on the final end of the game. Of course, to attempt to nullify this strategy, the opposing team usually switch to the "front-end game," whereby they place their draws in front of the house and await a miss or direct-on hit. This leaves them the opportunity to draw in behind the guard.

84

It is evident that strategy can be extremely complex and varied. Each situation demands the imagination and judgment of the skip in regard to his team members' strengths and the opposition's weaknesses. Thus it is necessary that a skip develop a deep insight into the game and have the confidence and ability to call and execute a game under the pressures of competition.

The following is a brief review of some basic situations the skip might consider.

I   DURING EARLY STAGES OF A GAME

1. If possible, have lead play both turns during first and second ends.
2. Watch own and opposition's rocks carefully at **all** times.
2. First few ends concentrate on watching each rock played for direction only. Let sweepers judge weight. (Read the ice.)
4. Make mental notes of every shot.
5. Experiment with draw shots by your lead or second over unplayed area to guard against a roll to that area by your opponent.
6. Watch your game continually, the ice might change during the game.

II.   JUDGING WEIGHT AND DIRECTION

Stand or crouch at tee on line of direction until shot is completed. Leave your post only on these occasions:

1. Simple draw, where weight is the only consideration.
2. To help pull a guard over the last few inches.

85

3. To get a guard over the hog line.
4. To sweep behind tee.
5. To sweep own rocks that are moved by unforeseen situations.

III.   PLAYING FIRST END

1. Place it on the rings. Reason: When you have last rock, it is advisable to keep front of house open.

   a. helps lead get feel of draw weight immediately.
   b. puts other skip on defensive.
   c. if opposition misses, you have a chance to draw in second shot.
   d. learn more about the ice.

2. Place it in front of the rings. Reason: When the opposition has last rock, plug up the front to make draw difficult.

   a. good position for a raise into the house.
   b. worries opposition.
   c. if opposition are good hitters.

   NOTE: If placing in front of rings, it should be on center line about 3 or 4 feet in front of the house. (For a raise, guard, and can play either turn around it.)

IV.   WHEN TO DRAW

1. Draw when your opponent's rocks are in any of the following:

a. on the back ring.
b. in a pocket.
c. partially guarded.

V.   WHEN TO HIT

1. on frosty ice, or dirty ice.
2. on swingy or wet ice.
3. removing guards.
4. When rock is in 8-foot or better, or front half of house.

VI.   WHEN TO PLAY A RAISE

1. When ice is grooved or runs straight.
2. When opponent is shot and guarded by one of your rocks.
3. Remember: Long raises are very difficult. Frozen rocks provide opportunities that will get you out of many serious situations.

VII.   WHEN TO PLAY A ROLL

1. To keep from bunching your own rocks in the rings.
2. To bury your rock behind a guard.
3. To get your rock in front of opposing rocks for backing.
4. To execute a double take-out.
5. To roll to a position guarding another rock.
6. To change play from one side of the house to the other during the early part of the game, so that the skip will have difficulty in judging the run of the ice.

Bibliography

ASH, BILL
"Leave the Hack Smoothly." **The Curler** (March, 1967), 18.

BALDWIN, MATT
"How to Release the Turns." **The Curler** (March, 1968), 24.

BEAUCHAMP, PATRICIA
"Don't Step Down on Your Heel." **The Curler** (November, 1965), 34.

CHICAGO PARK DISTRICT
Winter Activities. Chicago: Chicago Park District, Burnham Park, 1937.

DAGG, LYALL
"Take Your Left Foot Straight Back and Not Off to the Side." **The Curler** (November, 1965), 34.

HANDFORD, MORLEY
"Make Sure Your Swing is an Extension of the Straight Line from the Skip's Broom." **The Curler** (November, 1965), 11.

HOBBS, WALTER
"Don't Twist the Handle." **The Curler** (October, 1966), 22.

HUDSON, BRUCE
"Don't Bend the Elbow." **The Curler** (January, 1966), 15.

HUSHAGAN, EARL
"Early Season Exercises." **The Curler** (August, 1967), 21.

JESSUP, ELON
Snow and Ice Sports. New York: E. P. Dutton and Company, 1923.

McCUBBIN, ROBERT
"Hitting the Broom.", "Line of Delivery." **The Curler** (January-February, 1969), 9, 11.

METCALF, BOB
"Use Finger Tip Control." **The Curler** (March, 1966), 19.

MURDOCK, ROSS
"The Art of Sweeping." **The Curler** (March, 1966), 20.

RAMSAY, TOM
"Put One Foot Forward for Better Balance." **The Curler** (November, 1966), 8.

RICHARDSON, ERNIE;
McKEE, JOYCE; and MAXWELL, DOUG
Curling. Toronto, Ontario: Thomas Allen Limited, 1962.

ROYAL CALEDONIAN CURLING CLUB
Annual of the Royal Caledonian Curling Club for 1961-62. Edinburgh: Stanley Press, 1961.

ROYAL ROADS MILITARY COLLEGE
Victoria, British Columbia.

SINGER, R. N.
Motor Learning and Human Performance. London: MacMillan Company, Collier-MacMillan Limited, 1968.

SOMERVILLE, BUD
"Complete Your Backswing." **The Curler** (March, 1966), 18.

THE CURLER
Volume 1, No. 3 (May, 1964), 18.

URSULIAK, WALLY
"How to be a Stronger Sweeper." **The Curler** (April, 1966), 10.

WALSH, BILL
"Position the Stone Correctly." **The Curler** (January, 1966), 14.

WATSON, KEN
Ken Watson on Curling. Vancouver, Toronto, Montreal: The Copp Clark Publishing Company, 1950.

WEYMAN, H. E.
An Analysis of the Art of Curling. Levis, P.Q., Canada: Weyman, 1942.